Beautiful America's

Portland

First Printing, February 1989
Published by Beautiful America Publishing Company
9725 S.W. Commerce Circle
Wilsonville, Oregon 97070

Library of Congress Cataloging in Publication Data
Beautiful America's Portland
1. Portland (Or.) — Description — Views. I. Coughlan,
David. II. Title.
F884.P843R84 1988   917.95'49   88-7499
ISBN 0-89802-535-4
ISBN 0-89802-534-6 (Paperback)

Portland's Waterfront Fountain

Beautiful America's

Portland

Featuring Craig Tuttle Photography

Text by Leslie Rule
Geographic Research Assistant
David Coughlan

Contents

Introduction

I call Portland home. I have to admit there was a time when I considered myself just a visitor here, homesick for my state across the Columbia River. Seattle born, I was certain I would not survive unless I daily inhaled the salty air of Puget Sound.

That was seven years ago.

They say that your body replaces itself tissue for tissue, skin layer for skin layer, every seven years. If that is true, then I have become almost a native-born Oregonian. A full quarter of my life, spent in a city that continually delights me with new sights and different facets every time I wander its streets.

Standing on the corner of First Avenue and Salmon Street, in front of the windows full of carousel ponies, I can shut my eyes and smell popcorn and espresso and roses and the rivers and the faintest wafting of fir pitch from the forests in the distance.

When I travel across the Marquam Bridge I am dazzled by the sight of Portland, like a picture in a pop-up-book, downtown leaps into view, each building crisply emerging as the scene unfolds. There is an uncluttered balance here, as if each structure were carefully placed into position to complement those around it. New architecture is effectively blended with the old, and enhanced by a textured backdrop of rolling forested hills.

Lovely in the daytime, the city is magic at night! Lights dance in the velvety, black Willamette River and laughter floats on the breeze. Rickshaw rides are offered by brawny legged young men who run so swiftly that passengers have the sense of flying. Music drifts from nightclubs which overflow with enthusiasts who are just as happy to dance outside on the sidewalk.

If you want wild nightlife, or just plain wildlife, you can find it in Portland. Serene stretches of sylvan land abound. One city park covers 6,000 acres of wilderness! Pockets of wooded area—solace for the soul—can be discovered throughout the city.

Portland is at the very heart of land so fertile that seeds grow wherever they light—from a crack in the sidewalk, a rooftop, or sometimes—when the air is just damp enough—from the dust on an abandoned car. Strawberries and greenbeans, nuts and peaches, rhododendrons and weeds, and roses, roses, roses burst forth from the rich earth.

Portland Skyline (Overleaf)

Perhaps some people back east still think Portland is populated with cowboys and lumberjacks. Maybe it is, but it is also full of attorneys, stockbrokers, naval architects and computer geniuses. Portland is cosmopolitan without being jaded, serious without taking itself too seriously—a city with an irrepressible sense of humor.

Researching this book was akin to a treasure hunt; I thought I had seen all of Portland, and yet I found hidden prizes I never knew existed—vast parks, hidden coves, secret gems of places seldom advertised, rarely discovered.

Most of all I found that Portlanders care about preserving the beauty of their city. Those who went before us saved the land and its riches for us to know. Those who cherish today's Portland are carefully protecting it for generations yet to come.

When my breath stops at a sudden glimpse of Mt. Hood or I marvel at the exquisite detail of historical New Market Theatre, or peer so intently at the orange bricks of Pioneer Courthouse Square that my neck begins to ache, I think how lucky I am to be here. Every city in America has its natives and its boosters, and that is how it should be; New York is brash and brilliant and ahead of the crowd, Chicago is busy and intent on connecting every corner of this country by rail or plane or boat, and New Orleans is a grand lady serving tea and pecan pie behind ornate iron fences on a hot afternoon. I see cities that way!

Portland is a lovely, youthful, woman—with, of course—roses in her cheeks, roses in her arms, and roses tucked in her luxuriant hair. Portland is gracious, friendly, and polite to strangers—but watch her closely.

She's winking at you.

Physical Setting

Portland, Oregon was born at the northern end of the Willamette Valley. Cradled at the confluence of two vital rivers, the Columbia and the Willamette, the infant city was destined to grow to a major metropolis. The Columbia River, once a passageway for early explorers, such as Lewis and Clark, today is an important shipping lane for inter-ocean commerce. The Columbia River's great size prompted the building of many dams, including the Bonneville Dam which is a major supplier of Portland's electricity.

The Willamette River is an equally valuable resource to Portland. The longest north flowing river in the continental United States, this river has long been considered the life blood of the fertile agricultural Willamette Valley. Portland grew up alongside the Willamette, and to this day the river seems a more integral part of the city than its larger and more famous cousin, the Columbia.

A rolling ridge of forested hills lazily stretches out on Portland's west horizon. Portlanders refer to this natural boundary as the West Hills. A broad, sweeping valley floor unravels at the foot of the West Hills and reaches east to the foot hills of the Cascade Mountains.

For many years two spectacular Cascade Mountains, Mt. Hood and Mt. St. Helens, seemed to vie for Portlanders' attention like two rivaling sisters. Residents engaged in firey debates over which mountain was more grand; Mt. Hood with her sharp angular majesty, or Mt. St. Helens with her perfect sloping symmetry.

After years of competition, it was as if Mt. St. Helens suspected that Mt. Hood was receiving more than her share of recognition. In a burst of jealous rage she tossed a tantrum that captured the entire nation's attention.

It was May 18th of 1980 when the volcano who had behaved in a polite lady-like manner for centuries, erupted furiously, spewing forth billowing, white cauliflower shaped clouds of ash. Thanks to the whims of the wind, Portlanders received only a mild dusting. But hundreds of miles away, Eastern Washington got the brunt of the mountain's wrath when residents were literally buried to their knees in the noxious ash!

Portlanders dashed for their cameras and snapped away rolls of photos to record the rare geological occurrence. And entrepreneurs set up souvenir stands to sell bottled ash, posters and t-shirts. But as the excitement waned, so did the novelty of Mt. St. Helens. Her top half blown away, she is a shadow of her former self—a deflated mound in the distance.

It is Mt. Hood who snatches your breath away. She is the crowning glory on Portland's eastern horizon. Your eye naturally gravitates to Mt. Hood, who now wins the competition hands down.

Pittock Mansion

The Japanese Gardens

From Portland, calls of the wild lure day-trippers in every direction. Mt. Hood, the vast Pacific Ocean, rivers and forested wilderness are all within a hundred mile radius of the city. Beachcombers, skiers, campers and rafters can reach their respective destinations on half a tank of gas.

While many Portlanders admire Mt. Hood from afar, those who make the 60 mile trek to the mountain discover a variety of recreational activities. At 11,245 feet, this mountain is the highest peak in Oregon and features three complete ski areas for both Alpine and Nordic skiers. Mt. Hood is also the site of the enchanting Timberline Lodge, a choice get-away for skiers. Dedicated in 1937 by Franklin D. Roosevelt, this massive lodge is constructed of hand-hewn timbers, and enriched with carvings, paintings and mosaics by great American artists. Timberline's Palmer Chair Lift makes this resort the only one in North America which operates in summer and winter.

North of Mt. Hood, the Columbia River has carved a magnificent passage through the Cascade Mountains, creating one of the Northwest's most inspiring geological wonders—the Columbia River Gorge. Hikers delight in Multnomah Falls and numerous other spectacular waterfalls that spill over the rocky, mossy terrain.

The Gorge is also one the world's best wind-surfing sites. Thousands flock each year to Hood River and other Gorge cities to catch the wind in their colorful sails.

If you prefer a bigger body of water, the Pacific Ocean lies along the magical Oregon Coast, only 70 miles west of Portland. Its miles of rugged beach and exhilarating, pure, fresh air is all open to the public. With a bit of exploring you can find an expanse of uninhabited beach for private soul searching. Or, if you are feeling sociable, there are a number of peopled areas stocked with quaint shops and restaurants in the string of intriguing towns that edge the coastline.

You can engage in a variety of activities along the coast, including kite flying, beachcombing and wading. But beware of floating driftwood and capricious waves. Calm seas can suddenly give birth to treacherous undertow—dangerous even to strong swimmers. The Peter Iredale shipwreck serves as a warning that man is not always victorious when challenging the powerful sea. This barnacle covered hulk, imbedded on the beach of Fort Stevens Park since 1906, is just one of the fascinating things to see along the coast.

Portland is indeed blessed with a great diversity of natural environments within a short distance of the city. Skeptics, however, have been known to smugly question how Portlanders can enjoy the outdoors if it rains all of the time.

There are two answers to this question. First, it does not rain all of the time—just most of the winter. And secondly, Portlanders never let a little thing like rain interfere with their fun.

In defense of our climate, nearly half of Portland's 38 inches of annual rainfall occurs during the three months of November, December and January, which means we get a lot of that wet stuff out of the way in a short period. These months are admittedly a bit bleak due to an 80 percent cloud cover but temperatures are relatively mild with only the occasional snowstorm or freezing spell.

In spring, the benefits of all that winter rain become gloriously apparent. The clean air, sweet, colorful flowers and lush vegetation blend together to make a sunny day in Portland a marvelous treat for all the senses!

Summers here offer what many consider to be the finest weather in the country. Conditions are nearly ideal with pleasantly warm temperatures, low humidity and little rainfall.

Autumn is a season that often seems to have a dual personality. This time of year can serve up an Indian Summer with warm clear days and crisp, cool nights or can prepare us for the upcoming winter with an early dousing of rainy weather.

If you are still skeptical about the virtues of Portland's weather, keep in mind that the city has fared well in objective evaluations of its climate. In fact, one edition of *Rand McNally's Places Rated Almanac* listed Portland as having the 11th best climate in the nation. It ranked the city a surprising six places higher than Honolulu, Hawaii and perhaps a not so surprising 275 cities above last place Fairbanks, Alaska.

(Opposite) U.S. Navy attends The Portland Rose Festival

Rose Festival time

Early History

Portland is one major American city whose entire history is within the scope of the photography era. When I see early photographs of Portland, it reminds me of looking at an adult's baby pictures. The tilt of the nose and the dimple are familiar, just as the slope of a hill and a dip in the landscape distinguish Portland in an old photo. Yet, there is something strangely unfamiliar about these pictures; the determined set of a pioneer woman's eyes, or the plain box-like houses that seem about to be swallowed by the enormous wilderness. These images sharply contrast the ones we know; pioneer grit is replaced with carefree laughter and early shelters could easily fit in the corner of any Portland skyscraper's lobby. When you look at the city today it is a challenge to imagine Portland when it was simply "The Clearing," but that is how it started.

The Clearing was an opening in a grove of maple and oak trees on the banks of the Willamette River. Indians paused to rest there during trading expeditions between Fort Vancouver and Oregon City. With each stop, The Clearing grew larger as trees were chopped down to nourish the roaring campfires.

In 1843, former Tennessean William Overton and New England's Asa Lovejoy jointly filed a "Tomahawk Claim" on the 640 acres encompassing The Clearing. Early in 1844 Overton sold his half of the claim to Francis W. Pettygrove, also of Oregon City. Lovejoy and Pettygrove then began their dreams of building a city. But for the luck of a flip of a penny, the book you are now reading would be titled *Beautiful America's Boston.* Lovejoy wanted to name the city after his home town, Boston, Massachusetts; while Pettygrove favored Portland for his own home town of Portland, Maine. Portland won in two out of three tosses!

Before the year was over, the two partners had erected Portland's first house. In the summer of 1845, Lovejoy and Pettygrove platted the townsite into sixteen blocks and four streets. They didn't bother to remove the tree stumps. People from neighboring towns laughed and nicknamed the new city "Little Stumptown."

In these early years Portland was confined to the west side of the Willamette River. As a separate settlement evolved east of the river primitive ferry services were devised. An early-day entrepreneur opened a ferry business with one canoe and decidedly sporadic

Portland at dawn

service! Then in 1848, Israel Mitchell established a regular ferry route and others soon followed suit. James B. Stephens, the man who planned the townsite on the east side of the Willamette, began operating a ferry across the river in the early 1850's. The east side was still a separate settlement from Portland, known as East Portland. The ferry traveled from the foot of Stark Street on the west side to Oak Street on the east side.

When Portland was officially incorporated as a city in January of 1851, it had a population just short of 700. Less than two dozen stores stood along the city's unpaved streets and plank sidewalks. Most residents lived in log cabins and unpainted wooden dwellings weathered to the grey shade of a winter sky. A dense forest surrounded the little city and wild animals howled in the night.

Historians theorize that the establishment of a tannery, the discovery of gold in California and the opening of Canyon Road were the three factors that led to the first real growth spurt of Portland. The tannery was the only one west of the Rocky Mountains, and it attracted patrons from all over the Northwest, luring business to the city. The California gold rush put Portland merchandise in great demand. Some Portlanders joined the rush, became rich and returned home triumphant to use their wealth to fortify business ventures in their city. Canyon Road allowed farmers from the Tualatin Valley to transport their produce to Portland. Portland had the perfect river location for the produce trade. While Oregon City and Milwaukie were too far up-river for deep-sea vessels, the settlements down-river from Portland were too far from farm country. Portland was it!

Portland's first church, built almost single-handedly by Methodist minister, The Reverend James H. Wilbur, opened in 1850. More schools and churches sprang up as the infant city's population grew.

A great interest in "culture" prevailed in Portland. Even in the 1850's, city folk eagerly attended musicals, plays, and concerts in such places as Portland's National Hall on Front Street and the Metropolitan Hotel. Patrons of literature drew several poets and writers to the city.

Portland boomed. In 1870, horse and mule-powered street cars ran on iron-railed tracks in the city's streets. A more sophisticated electric car replaced the animals in

March of 1890. Real estate values in the outlying areas increased substantially with faster, easier transportation.

These early years were marred, however, by disasters from two opposite forces, fire and water—elements which would prove to play integral roles in the shaping of Portland.

Portland merchants, their businesses perched on the river banks, grew used to the threat of floods. As the river rose, they habitually moved goods from basements to upper floors. Yet the flood of 1876 surprised everyone. It was June 9th when the water crept to street level. Within a few days the river lapped eagerly at the porch of the Cosmopolitan Hotel, and actually spilled over the first floor of the Clarendon Hotel!

Front Street merchants weighted their wooden sidewalks down with chains, kegs of nails and all the scrap iron they could lay their hands on. Wooden buildings were braced with strong pieces of timber to keep them from floating away. And the streets themselves were layered with bricks and gravel to prevent the pavement from drifting off.

In an effort to keep guests dry, the Clarendon Hotel raised its first floor above the water, and along the waterfront elevated sidewalks were built for pedestrians. Noting the precarious tilt of these makeshift walkways, the newspaper cautioned individuals who imbibed to avoid the flooded area of town. By the end of June, the water had receded and things were back to normal by July.

Four years later, on June 27th, 1880, another flood gushed, this time with Front Street overflowing from Washington to Glisan. Portland boys took advantage of the water, joyfully paddling around Front Street on rafts. With its first floor under water, The Oregonian newspaper prudently moved its business office to the second floor. By the first of July the water had reached its peak at 27.4 feet. The Clarendon Hotel's dining room was under five feet of water; the hotel's guests rode boats to and from their rooms!

The 1870's was also the period of Portland's most devastating fires. The first began in a Chinese laundry on a December morning in 1872. Several live coals, employed in the boiling of pitch, fell under the laundry and ignited lumber. Flames quickly shot up, and by the time fire engines arrived, a brisk wind had fanned the fire out of control. Many

Portland's geometric skyline

(Opposite) Skyline reflections

houses along the river rested on stilts, a precaution against floods that proved to be a catalyst to the fire. Flames slithered up the stilts and ignited the homes.

Unfortunately, the majority of the homes in the area were constructed of dry, light, highly flammable fir. As a south wind blew the fire north, many feared that the entire city would be lost. Emergency cisterns of water were depleted in two hours.

Telegraphic messages for help were dispatched to Vancouver, Oregon City, Salem, Albany and Eugene. By the afternoon several cities' fire departments had arrived to assist. Finally, the wind subsided and a heavy rain fell, squelching the last of the flames; but two and a half blocks were destroyed at an estimated loss of a half a million dollars.

Nine months later, on a dry August night in 1873, a fire started in a furniture store on First, near Taylor Street. The flames leapt from building to building, effortlessly spanning Portland's narrow streets. Again, help was requested from neighboring cities. As a Salem fire engine doused the fire with water from the Willamette River, the Protection Engine House on First and Jefferson burned to the ground.

Hotels, livery stables, stores, saloons and houses were among those consumed by the greedy flames. The intense heat even penetrated brick buildings, igniting their contents and melting glass windows.

The 1873 fire proved to be the worst in Portland's history, sweeping over 22 blocks, and destroying nearly every structure in its path! A loss of over two million dollars was estimated. Many of the merchants possessed little or no insurance. One vegetable merchant was unable to collect debts owed him; as all his records were written on the walls of his shop, destroyed in the fire.

Portland immediately began to rebuild. Many merchants moved back to the charred remains of their shops. Blackened debris was cleared out and tossed in the river as Portlanders began to pick up the pieces.

When we examine the ravages of floods and fires that Portland endured during the 1870's, it is amazing that the little city did not give up. Yet, as the 1870's saw Portland take a step backward due to natural disasters, it also saw a spirited city rebound two steps ahead, thanks to the construction of the railroad, an event that spawned growth outside of Portland's original boundaries and encouraged traveling to and from the burgeoning city.

Another major change occurred in Portland with the building of the first of many bridges. As early as the 1850's several attempts were made by different organizations to build a bridge across the Willamette River. None was successful until April of 1887, when the Morrison Street Bridge opened as a toll bridge. The fact it was a draw bridge, squelched opponents' fears that it would obstruct navigation. A pedestrian was allowed across for five cents, a driver and two horses for twenty cents and a nickel a piece was charged for a loose sheep or pig.

Four years later, in 1891, Portland and East Portland officially became one city!

Downtown

Nestled between the west hills and the Willamette River, downtown Portland is a geometrical treat for the eye—buildings of many shapes and sizes blend together in an exciting potpourri of architecture. From nearly every angle you can find a pleasing collage of angular structures which overlap, parallel, and backdrop one another as they carve out shapes in the sky.

Like faces in a family album, buildings from every era of Portland's history remind us of our past. The elegant and ornate structures from the 1880's stand side by side with the streamlined skyscrapers of a century later. A stroll through the downtown area is rich with history and character.

Many of Portland's oldest buildings are located in the Skidmore/Old Town area which covers twenty city blocks. Old Town contains many brick and cast iron structures which retain some interesting testimony to Portland's past. The Haseltine Building, on Second and Pine, was built in 1893 and recalls the major flood of 1894. The Willamette's high watermark is still recorded on one of the building's recessed doorways.

The Yamhill Historic District, adjacent to Old Town, is near the south end of the heart of Portland's early commercial area. When the devastating fires of the 1870's destroyed most of the early buildings in the Yamhill District, prominent businessmen built new High Victorian Italianate structures with ornamental cast iron facades. Many of these still stand today.

The Portland Building and "Portlandia"

KOIN Building

Orbanco Building

While the Willamette River, touted as "Portland's Highway," was the very thing that originally made the city an enticing place, it was also responsible for driving Portland's business core up to higher, dryer ground. The 1894 flood destroyed a gas system, undermined building foundations and coated the area with mud and debris.

The concentration of glazed terra cotta buildings, erected between 1905 and 1930, begins several blocks west from the river in the present downtown center. Terra cotta buildings can be recognized by their beige or off-white color and by lavish detail, such as the eagles, griffins, lions' heads and classical motifs which adorn them. A series of glazed terra cotta structures, many designed by noted Portland architects Doyle, Patterson and Beach, were built along the major downtown street car lines.

Critically acclaimed Portland architect Pietro Belluschi left his mark on Portland with such structures as the Museum Building and the Commonwealth Building. The Commonwealth Building on Sixth Avenue—formerly known as the Equitable Building—was constructed in 1948 and is the first in the world to employ the glass curtain wall. The unadorned, sleek glass exterior of Belluschi's design soon became characteristic of buildings worldwide.

In recent years skyscrapers have sprouted in Portland, a sight pioneers could never have imagined; the First Interstate Tower, dubbed "The Ivory Tower" because of its cream colored stone, offers a breathtaking panoramic view of the city from its 21st story restaurant. Another of Portland's tallest buildings, the U.S. Bancorp Tower, stands out from the crowd with its polished pink exterior and reflecting glass. Atwater's, a renowned Portland restaurant, offers a spectacular view from the top of this building.

Noted Portland architect, Robert Frasca, has contributed considerably to Portland's skyline with such structures as the Willamette Center, Franklin Plaza, and the Justice Center. Perhaps most noticeable on the skyline is Frasca's KOIN Center with its orange brick and ziggurat appearance.

Michael Graves's Portland Building, located on Fifth Avenue is the first major post modernistic structure in America, and serves as a throne for Portlandia. This giant, hammered copper lady, sculpted by Raymond Kasky, caught the nation's attention when she came to Portland in 1986. The last leg of Portlandia's journey from Washington D.C. was quite an event as she traveled by barge four and a half miles up the river. Hundreds of people boarded yachts, tugboats, canoes and kayaks to welcome her and thousands more lined the streets to greet the shimmering statue. Patinating with time, Portlandia has lost that new penny glimmer but her gradually deepening shade adds warmth to the gracious statue. She leans toward awed pedestrians below, extending her hand in welcome.

The varied facades of Portland's buildings are more than just so many pretty faces. All downtown buildings are required to have ground level activity space to allow for personal interaction with the city's residents. Shoppers delight in the abundance of specialty shops, quaint eateries and interesting galleries.

One of the more intriguing places to shop in Portland is the New Market Theatre. The elegant historical structure at 50 S.W. Second Avenue debuted in 1872 as a celebrated theatre. Thirty-five foot high ceilings, plush, red velvet box seats, hundreds of gas lights and a balcony all contributed to its reputation as "the finest theatre in the West!"

Two decades later, however, the curtain descended on this splendid theatre. Following the demise of founder Alexander Ankeny in 1891, the legendary theatre was cast in a series of humbling roles: a warehouse, a storage building and a parking garage, her red plush seats and bright lights gone.

Happily, today the New Market Theatre is back in the spotlight. It made its comeback in 1982 when Portlanders came to their senses and restored the grand structure, officially declaring it a historical site. Much of the charm and character of the original theatre has been retained. An airy promenade, graced with bold cast iron columns, serves as the central pathway to the cluster of specialty shops and restaurants nestled within its walls. This beautiful theatre deserves a standing ovation for its belated encore.

The reincarnation of historical buildings as shopping malls is a popular theme in Portland. The Galleria, on S.W. Ninth and Alder, boasting nearly 50 shops and restaurants, began as the Olds and King Department store in 1905. The Johns Landing Water Tower, located just south of downtown Portland, was originally a furniture factory, built in 1903. Today it is home to over 45 stores and restaurants and can be easily recognized by the retired water tower hovering above it.

River Place Marina at night

(Opposite) Tom McCall Waterfront Park

The Saturday Market is the best place to shop for unique items. The weekend, open-air market, established in 1974, is located in downtown Portland under the Burnside Bridge. Artists, craftspeople and entrepreneurs rent space in the 300 booths that make up the seasonal market. The choices are tempting with a wide selection of handmade goods. Pottery, paintings, toys, jewelry and furniture are all exquisitely crafted. Just strolling among the booths, your senses are delightfully inundated with the wide spectrum of vivid colors, the rich scents of ethnic (and familiar) foods, and stray notes from street musicians mingling with the chattering crowds.

Interestingly, Saturday Market recalls another market of an earlier era. Yamhill Street, just eight blocks away from the Saturday Market, was the site of a similar market which opened in 1914. The Caroll Public Market covered a six block area, where 400 farmers sold their goods from tables and wagons. Portlanders flocked to the market to buy tomato plants, dressed rabbit, apples, berries and butter. There was an international flavor to the market, as many of the merchants were of Oriental, Italian and Northern European descent.

Business was so brisk in 1914 at the popular market that Yamhill Street became useless as a thoroughfare. Eventually—to clear up Yamhill, and to provide essential jobs in the Depression—a long-planned Public Market Building was sanctioned by the city. The indoor market opened in December of 1933. But Portlanders missed their open-air market and the new market never really caught on. The color and ambiance was not there and it closed after only a decade.

Apparently, some things never change. The thousands of people who visit the Saturday Market are testimony to the fact that Portlanders from all eras prefer their markets open-air.

Chinatown is another spot which evokes nostalgia for Portland's past. Located in the Old Town section of downtown, it is an integral part of the city's history. At one time Portland had one of the largest Oriental settlements in the country, second only to San Francisco. It was a city within a city, with an approximate population of 10,000. Many of the Chinese were attracted by the California gold rush and traveled to California from their home country. Later they came to Portland by steamship. For many years they wore the traditional Chinese loose-flowing garb along with a queue, the single braid hanging from the back of the head.

Although Chinatown today is considerably smaller, with only a few Chinese restaurants and shops to distinguish it from the rest of the city, it is recognized as having important historical significance in the shaping of Portland. In 1986 the China Gate, which spans Fourth Avenue at Southwest Burnside, was dedicated as part of the revitalization program for the Old Town/Chinatown district, as well as to commemorate the 135 year contribution from the Chinese culture to the area. An impressive structure, the brightly colored gate is of authentic Chinese construction and design, graced with five roofs, 64 dragons and two imposing bronze lions.

Downtown Portland is generously laced with open spaces. City planners must have shuddered at the thought of densely packed buildings squeezing out the sunshine. Careful plotting of light inviting spaces allows plants and humans alike to thrive in the sunlight. Primroses, pansies and geraniums flourish from March to September in huge concrete planters that line the city's sidewalks, and year-round sidewalk vendors peddling espresso, pretzels or flowers can enjoy a little sun too.

One of the area's more popular open spaces is Pioneer Courthouse Square located in the heart of downtown. Portland architect Willard Martin visualized "a downtown living room for the people of Portland" when he designed the Square. The plaza is named for the Pioneer Courthouse which sits grandly across the street on Sixth Avenue, overlooking the Square. Built in 1873, the courthouse is the Pacific Northwest's oldest public building.

Opened to the public in April of 1981, the Square has become a place where folks go to relax, eat a sack lunch, people-watch, or to attend one of the hundreds of scheduled events. Fairs, exhibits, spontaneous orations or lunch hour concerts are always on the agenda at the Square.

Pioneer Courthouse Square has its own unique character. Many benches, whimsical sculptures and a mile post are integrated into the plaza's design. A water fountain of

New Market Theater and U.S. Bancorp Tower

purple hued tiles is a surprisingly perfect foil for the orange brick of the Square.

Sometimes the Square seems more like Portland's rumpus room than its living room, due to the spirited youth who frequent it. Portlanders seem to truly enjoy the Square. The fact that 11,000 people showed up to see the lighting of the Square's Christmas tree attests to their interest and enjoyment.

Much of the Square's success can be attributed directly to Portland's citizens. More than half a million dollars was collected for the Square's funding when personalized bricks were "sold" in 1981. Those who paid a fee to have their names etched on the bricks can often be seen, wandering around the Square with bowed heads hoping to spot their names among the thousands of others.

Tom McCall Waterfront Park is another wide open space in the downtown core and a great location for a stroll along the Willamette River. While other cities have been known to bulldoze through parks and forests to make way for freeways, Portland, in a delightfully "backward" action removed a major freeway corridor to make room for this park in the early 1970's. Completed in 1977, the park was recently renamed in honor of Portland's late Governor McCall, a dedicated conservationist, who led efforts to clean up the Willamette River.

The beautifully landscaped 23-acre park borders the Willamette River. Adjacent to the park, the shops, restaurants and hotels of the Riverplace Marina complex have been gracefully integrated into the waterfront setting. You can choose to dine, jog along the promenade, watch the boats go by, or just sit and gaze at the park's spectacular fountain. The spigot of the $260,000 fountain was officially turned on in May of 1988. Featuring five displays which change every eight seconds, the fountain is especially magical to watch at night as it sends lighted jets of water shooting in all directions.

Her citizens' fondness for parks was apparent early in Portland's history. The Park Blocks, a 25 block area between Park and Ninth Avenues was set aside in 1852 for the "enjoyment of the people!" Nicknamed "The Boulevard," the Blocks became a place for early townspeople and traders to congregate. Like a tranquil island, the Park Blocks are a contrast to the bustling activity of the surrounding city. The elm trees, offering shade in the summer, drop their leaves in the fall, providing a brilliant carpet of gold.

The Arlene Schnitzer Concert Hall

"The Schnitz"

Concert Hall Chandelier

In addition to its transcendent beauty, Portland is an incredibly whimsical place and fanciful touches can be found throughout the downtown area. A menagarie of wild creatures gambol and forage in the fountains along Southwest Morrison and Yamhill Streets. The bronze animals are a complete surprise, totally unexpected on a city street. Sculpted by northwest artist Georgia Gerber, the 25 figures of native Oregon wildlife are pleasing to the eye and inviting to the touch. Children love to pet the cool smooth forms, while adults enjoy a tranquil moment listening to the gentle splashing of the fountains' waters.

Folks traveling along Taylor Street do a double-take the first time they glimpse the south side of the Taylor Building. Three goats balance precariously from window ledges on the historical building! Actually, the goats are paintings, but they appear three dimensional, due to the artfully applied shadows.

Downtown Portland is a work of art, shaped by the combined efforts of Mother Nature and talented architects, sculptors and artists, but—most of all—by generations of Portlanders. From the sparkling Willamette River to the graceful form of Portlandia to the mischievous goats climbing the Taylor Building, something lovely or enchanting is sure to be found around every corner in downtown Portland.

Westside

West Portland is a lush, flowing land of hills and valleys. Like a roller coaster, the landscape ambles lazily along, in places climbing suddenly to a rounded crest before falling away to lowland.

Millions of trees make the west side of the city a squirrel haven. In parts the trees stand so close that their branches connect, creating a virtual squirrel freeway high in the tree tops. The energetic little creatures can scamper for miles without touching the ground!

Many of the westside's older residential areas remain densely wooded, with meandering streets and secluded homesites. Towering firs and pines have been allowed to thrive and the neighborhoods have been carefully integrated into this natural setting.

Rising abruptly from downtown, the forested west hills contain some of Portland's most exclusive neighborhoods, long considered residential enclaves for Portland's more prosperous citizens. Palatial homes tucked into the hillside offer commanding views of the city below.

At the foot of the west hills and bordering the downtown area, northwest Portland is one of the oldest and most intriguing neighborhoods. A diverse range of people, including artists, writers and young professionals reside in this charming section of town. A sunny afternoon finds a jean clad novelist typing from his porch "office" while next door a young lawyer, briefcase in hand, stops to pull a weed as she heads for court.

The distinct flavor of the area is due in part to its scores of Victorian houses. Many have been renovated in recent years and reflect a new pride in the neighborhood. Painted colors from canary yellow to deepest purple, to more subtle tones of beige and brown, these historical homes mirror the diverse personalities of their inhabitants.

The Lair Hill section, located just south of downtown, is another area of historical significance. In recent years a concerted effort was made to restore and preserve this working class neighborhood. To assure the preservation of these classic, vintage homes, the residents of Lair Hill successfully lobbied to have their neighborhood designated a historic conservation district. As a result, Lair Hill today is a charming, special place, as it was in the past.

The exclusive Dunthorpe neighborhood, located in southwest Portland, offers its residents a rural setting, yet is situated just minutes from downtown Portland. A view of the Willamette River, a natural wooded environment and stately homes combine to make this one of the most desirable areas in the city to live.

In 1871 the city of Portland purchased a 145 acre expanse of land in the west hills with no immediate plans for its future. It proved to be a wise purchase. Today, this section of

Union Station

Reed College

forested land above the city is Washington Park. Many of Portland's cultural attractions are located here, such as the Japanese Gardens, Pittock Mansion and the Washington Park Zoo, to name a few.

With something for everyone, the park is alive with activity. An outdoor amphitheatre showcases a series of entertaining musical and theatre productions staged by the Portland Park Bureau each summer. Near the theatre, a Shakespearean garden blossoms forth with all the flowers and foliage referred to in the playwright's works—a garden out of time and place, mythical and charming!

The athletically inclined can choose from tennis courts to archery ranges, or merely enjoy running, bicycling or strolling along the winding roads which lead to the park's other attractions.

A springtime favorite at Washington Park, the International Rose Test Gardens, founded in 1917, are the oldest continuously operating test gardens in the country. Seven decades of roses! The intricate gardens cover four and a half acres with 400 varieties of roses planted on three manicured terraces. In addition to roses, visitors to this site are also treated to a marvelous view of the city, considered by many to be the ultimate vista in Portland.

The Japanese Gardens are a wonderfully serene environment with sculpted shrubs, trickling waterfalls, and ponds alive with colorful fish. Increased trade and cultural interaction with Japan prompted the opening of the Gardens in 1963. Acclaimed as one of the most authentic of its kind outside of Japan, this attraction is actually a network of gardens, each with a distinct theme. Fixtures and lanterns were imported from Japan, but shrubs, trees and stones were acquired locally. An incredible view of Portland, backdropped by Mt. Hood compliments the tranquil beauty of the gardens.

The award winning Washington Park Zoo constantly tops itself as it adds new and exciting natural habitat exhibits to its expanding facility. The zoo's roots go back to the early 1880's when a Morrison Street druggist purchased a grizzly and an Alaskan bear from a visiting sailor for a total of a hundred and twenty-five dollars. He then presented them to the city. A zoo was born!

Washington Park Zoo gives new meaning to the term "wild party" each April as they celebrate the birthday of their favorite zoo celebrity: Packy! This elephant made national news in 1962 when he became the first Asian elephant born in the Western Hemisphere.

Today, Portland's zoo boasts the world's largest captive elephant herd with the birth of over two dozen bouncing baby pachyderms since Packy. But Packy still holds a special place in Portlanders' hearts. Moved by memories of the elephant's birth, one dedicated elephantophile recently donated $100,000.00 toward renovation of the elephants' quarters and an elephant museum!

Elephants aren't the only large attraction at the Washington Park Zoo. Daily visitors delight in watching the penguins' underwater antics through the glass wall which reveals the Humboldt Penguin Exhibit. This exhibit replicates the coastline of Peru, complete with rolling waves. The Alaska Tundra exhibit features bears, musk oxen, snowy owls and lemmings—a cool view on a hot summer day!

For a great ride, hop aboard the zoo train for a round trip excursion through the west hills to the Japanese Gardens.

The summer season at the zoo offers many musical moods for the receptive throngs who gather on the lawn to lounge and listen to weekly blue grass, big band and jazz concerts.

Two other popular westside attractions are located in Washington Park. The World Forestry Center and OMSI are literally just a stone's throw away from the Zoo.

OMSI (short for Oregon Museum of Science and Industry) is a favorite of the imaginative and curious of mind. Here you can explore a wide variety of fascinating displays. Imagine a gigantic walk-through heart, a transparent talking woman and the cutting edge of the computer age! From the enormous automated dinosaurs to Jim Henson's Muppet display, the ever-changing exhibits not surprisingly attract all age groups.

OMSI was born entirely from volunteers' donations. Originally constructed in 1957, the entire exterior structure was erected by 400 volunteers in a single day! Today, the museum is still self-supporting, funded by memberships, donations, grants and admission fees. A visit to the World Forestry Center will involve you in one of Oregon's most

First Christian Church

The Old Church

First Congregational Church

vital natural resources. A seventy-foot tall, talking tree greets visitors to the center. A display of every significant tree species indigenous to North America, a forest fire dramatization and a simulated paper mill are included in these interesting and educational exhibits.

The Pittock Mansion is a short drive from the World Forestry Center. This mansion is named for an early publisher of Portland's prominent newspaper, The Oregonian. Henry Pittock chose a spot for his extravagant home high atop a majestic hill on Portland's west side in 1909. After five years of construction, the mansion was completed. Elegant and superbly crafted, the home boasts imported marble, cut stone and exotic woods. Crystal chandeliers, an ornately flanked winding marble staircase and an oval room all contribute to the grandeur of the structure. Visitors are spellbound by the gorgeous view of the city. The Pittocks enjoyed a decade of spectacular mornings when brilliant golden sunrises swept over the Willamette and Columbia Rivers and sparkled on the mountains beyond.

After Henry Pittock's death in 1919 at age 83, heirs found the huge house to be a cumbersome and costly burden. It suffered neglect until 1964 when Portland citizens rallied to its plight and raised funds for the mansion's purchase. Today, it is the property of the Portland Bureau of Parks and Recreation and is open nearly every afternoon for public viewing.

While the west hills boast many man-made attractions, none can rival what nature has done. Forest Park is a 6,000 acre wilderness area, a generous slice of solitude just three miles from the hustle-bustle of downtown Portland. Thirty miles of paths wind, climb and dip over the wooded ridge which separates the Tualatin Valley from the Willamette River.

Early developers' plans were thwarted when they discovered it would be too expensive to bring utilities to the rugged terrain. City planners had recommended the area for a municipal forest park as early as 1903, and in 1947 it was finally declared an official public park. The land has had a history of fires, with the last major fire in 1951 when an abandoned campfire ignited the woods. It quickly grew to a ravenous, angry blaze which swept over 1200 acres and burned for three days, prompting the city to take new measures for fire prevention.

Today the land has recovered, with towering firs, bigleaf maples and alders abounding. Wildflowers such as Oregon grape, fireweed and delicate fairy lanterns brighten the paths when in season. A lucky hiker may catch a rare glimpse of the grazing deer who make their home in the beautiful wooded park—along with coyotes, bobcat and beaver.

Council Crest is another park with a story behind it. With a zenith of 1,073 feet, Council Crest is the highest point of the city. Portland traded an old firehouse for the land in 1937, and in turn received one of the most magnificent views of Portland and the surrounding area. Choose a clear day to examine the park's huge brick compass and gaze out at five Cascade Mountain peaks!

Several miles southeast from Council Crest, Tyron Creek State Park offers a more "down to earth" perspective of Portland. Tyron Creek Canyon was logged in the 1880's by the Oregon Iron Company to provide fuel for the iron smelter in Lake Oswego. Replenished naturally over the years, the forest now is a dense mix of red alder, Douglas fir, bigleaf maple and western red cedar trees. The 641 acre park contains eight miles of hiking trails, three and a half miles of horse trails and three miles of bicycle trails. Wildlife flourishes here with over eighty species of birds and numerous small animals who call the park home.

Eastside

Portland is not one but two cities, divided by the Willamette River, but linked by many bridges. Cultural as well as topographical differences distinguish the two sides of the city. A good natured rivalry sometimes surfaces, perhaps stemming back to the era when Portland and East Portland were indeed two separate settlements. Over a century ago the two sides competed in the building of a railroad, each laying its own separate track!

Jackson Tower

"Allow Me" Statue and Christmas Tree, Pioneer Courthouse Square

"The square" in use

East Portland, sharply contrasting the west side's rolling terrain, sits on a broad, flat plain stretching eastward to the foothills of the Cascade Mountains. Rising above the plain is Mt. Tabor, the only extinct volcano located within a continental U.S. city. The north end of the mountain's crater is encircled by an outdoor amphitheatre.

Rocky Butte, another arresting interruption to the plain, was once the site of the Multnomah County Jail. A winding road leads to the top of the butte where you can gaze over the roof tops across the city and observe the landings and take offs of planes from Portland International Airport.

Eastside neighborhoods have a very distinct urban flavor. Grid street patterns, the close proximity of houses to each other, sidewalks and established older homes all give a sense of living in the midst of a city rather than a suburb. Yet, the east side is threaded with gracious neighborhoods of fine homes such as Laurelhurst, Eastmoreland and Ladd's Addition.

Ladd's Addition, a planned neighborhood plotted against the grain of the rest of the city's streets, looks a little like a spiderweb on the city map. A park-like garden sits in the center and a series of streets splay out, eventually being criss-crossed by more streets. Gardens of roses, azaleas and rhododendrons, incorporated into the symmetrical pattern, are a source of pride to the peaceful neighborhood. Lawns and homes are well tended and a quiet sense of dignity prevails throughout. This uniquely designed neighborhood was built largely in the 1910's and 1920's, and today is a historical conservation district.

The Laurelhurst section boasts some of Portland's most sumptuous homes. Ornate mansions with sweeping lawns and sculpted hedges, grace the neighborhood's curving roads. Other, less ostentatious, but still tenderly cared-for houses, share this southeast portion of the city. Many young families inhabit the bungalows and 1920 vintage box-like homes which are also part of the area's flavor.

Laurelhurst Park, in the very heart of the eastside is cherished by folks throughout the area. The park which covers ten city blocks, was planned and designed in the early 1900's, making it one of the city's oldest parks. Today, joggers pound along the wide paths, enjoying the lush terrain.

"The Coming of the Whiteman" Statue, Washington Park

Serene Plaza

"The Thompson Elk" and Portland Building

Metropolitan Area Express—"Max"

Portland's Center for the Performing Arts

Neighborfair

Reflections in glass

One Financial Center

Perfect specimen

Portland Rose Test Gardens

Crystal Springs Rhododendron Gardens

Washington Park Zoo

One of the inhabitants

Oregon Museum of Science and Industry—OMSI

The China Gate

Artquake's grass people

Colorful street stands

"Here comes the parade"

Indian Maiden

Portland Rose Festival Parade

Beautiful floats

The end

The focal point of the park is Laurelhurst Pond. Geese and ducks are a treat to watch as they glide over the water, occasionally turning bottoms up as they forage for food. Rhododendrons, azaleas, camellias and cherry trees add brilliant color and sweet aroma to the park in the spring. Easter services in this inspiring setting have attracted crowds for many years.

The Grotto, located several miles northeast of Laurelhurst Park, is another sylvan location for outdoor church services. Inspired by a Catholic priest's vision, the sanctuary was established in 1924. The Grotto is named for the cave carved into the face of a 110 foot cliff which enshrines a white marble replica of Michelangelo's Pieta.

A ten-story elevator connects the two levels of the Grotto. High on the cliff a meandering path leads visitors through a peaceful garden of splendid flowering shrubs, fountains, ponds and holy shrines graced by exquisite marble sculptures. Redwood trees imported decades ago as seeds, mingle with the Northwest's natural firs and pines.

On the lower level, the chapel is a work of art, with its brass doors, 25 foot high stained glass windows and lovely murals. The outside services are held in the warmer months, May to September in the awe-inspiring outdoor cathedral. Visitors of every faith are welcome to explore all 64 acres of the tranquil woods and pastoral gardens of this beautiful Catholic sanctuary.

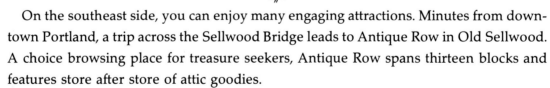

On the southeast side, you can enjoy many engaging attractions. Minutes from downtown Portland, a trip across the Sellwood Bridge leads to Antique Row in Old Sellwood. A choice browsing place for treasure seekers, Antique Row spans thirteen blocks and features store after store of attic goodies.

Part of the charm of Antique Row is that business is conducted in an old neighborhood setting, with most of the shops located in the homes and stores of a bygone era. If it weren't for the signs out front, you might assume that you were in a proud neighborhood rather than a great place to shop! This feeling carries over into the shops, many of them family owned and operated. People come from great distances to buy, browse, dicker or trade, with plenty of chatter and smiles.

If nourishment is required after a hard day of bargain hunting, there are many superb eateries sprinkled among the shops. While some of these restaurants feature ethnic food and exotic desserts, others have retained a homey feel, serving hearty soups and fresh baked cookies. Some of the later conduct business under the very roofs where families once lived. The cozy informal ambience gives you the sense of dropping in on friendly strangers for a home-cooked meal.

Very close to Antique Row, at the east end of the Sellwood Bridge, Oaks Park is set in a beautiful wooded area that stretches into 44 acres along the Willamette River. Opened in 1905 to coincide with the Lewis and Clark World's Exposition, the non-profit park has picnic areas, seasonal amusement rides and the biggest indoor roller skating rink in the Pacific Northwest.

The Herschel Spillman Carousel adds to the old-fashioned ambience of Oaks Park. Constructed in 1911, it was relocated to the park in 1923 and has been merrily going around ever since. The brightly colored and bejeweled carousel includes pigs, cats, dogs, a rooster, an ostrich and rabbits, along with the much-loved painted ponies. Through-out the years, thousands of children have made mad dashes for their favorite animal on this enchanting musical menagerie.

Oaks Park has always been an entertaining place. In the early part of the century, vaudeville shows were popular at the park. Later, an electric trolley connected Oaks Park and Portland, and in the summer band concerts were held in a large white gazebo. Portlanders clapped to the music of John Phillip Sousa or toe-tapped to an authentic German band. Today, the Ladybug Theatre, a children's participatory group, is a recom-mended family attraction with its everchanging array of humorous presentations.

The river beach is a bonus at Oaks Park. You can take pathways from the picnic grounds to the water's edge for a peaceful stroll along the river. The river traffic and the view of the Portland skyline makes this a memorable stop.

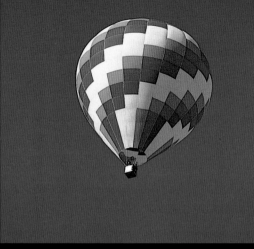

Sailing on the Columbia

Culture and Events

"It's my party and I'll cry if I want to!" could be Portland's theme song with her reputation for untimely outbursts of rain during the city's biggest party of the year—the June Rose Festival. Despite this, Portlanders' enthusiasm is not "dampened" by the inclement weather. Each year, thousands take part in the three weeks of celebration, highlighted with parades, a carnival in Tom McCall Waterfront Park, outdoor concerts, with crowning of a Rose Queen and hot air balloon and world class auto races.

The origins of the Rose Festival can be traced back to the pioneer era when traders carried seeds of the wild rose from England to the Pacific Northwest. Oregon Trail immigrants crossing the plains with ox teams brought precious rose bushes and planted them in the new land. Cuttings were eagerly snipped from the original bushes, and these were lovingly tucked into flower beds alongside the log cabins. As the roses and the pioneers thrived, the sturdy flower soon became a symbol of the growing city of Portland.

It was 1888 when Mrs. Henry Pittock placed a large canopy on the lawn at her home on Tenth and Washington and invited friends and neighbors to exhibit their roses in her pavilion. C. E. S. Wood, a local poet, was so enamored with the beauty of the fragrant rose that he suggested the city hold an annual rose show. A few years later, members of the Oregon Historical Society began promoting Portland as "The Rose City." Then in 1905, Harry Lane, the mayor of Portland, publicly proclaimed the city should have a festival of roses.

The idea grew and in 1907 Portland's first Rose Festival and Floral Parade was held with thousands of people lining the streets to see the two mile procession of flower laden autos and horse-and-buggies. Enthusiastic Portlanders piled their vehicles high with enormous bouquets of roses. Store fronts were decked out with flowers, and the Forestry Building was festooned with a solid bank of roses stretching all the way around the massive structure. Each one of the millions of roses decorating the city was picked from a Portland garden, and the newspapers declared that "Stumptown" had truly earned her new title as "The Rose City" with her impressive display of the regal flower.

This early tribute to the Rose has blossomed into Portland's annual showcase, The Grand Floral Parade; now nationally televised and ranked as one of the largest events of its kind in the world.

In 1918, a group of enterprising east Portland youngsters decided to form their own parade, decorating their doll buggies and wagons with ribbons and flowers. The children's charm and ingenuity were an immediate success and in 1936, the Junior Rose Parade became an official part of the Rose Festival. Today, over 10,000 children, along with a fair share of ponies and dogs, join in this lively event, billed as the largest of its kind in the country.

With the addition of the Starlight Parade, Rose Festival Queens and Junior Queens, and a century of fragrant summers later, one can only imagine Mrs. Pittock's reaction had she known the "rosy future" her little garden show would inspire in Portland.

Roses are not the only reason that Portlanders can find for a party! Visitors here soon learn that this is a city that likes to celebrate. Fun ranks high on Portland's list of priorities. Downtown Portland, especially, seems to take on an almost carnival atmosphere with a continuous parade of fun events scheduled for her people's pleasure. An air of excitement and enthusiasm prevails with each approaching event.

The Tom McCall Waterfront Park is a favorite location for many fairs, concerts and shows. In addition to serving as the site of the Rose Festival carnival, the park also plays host to such events as Neighborfair, the Portland Blues Festival and The Waterfront Classics. The latter are noon concerts performed by the Oregon Symphony Orchestra and are free to the public.

Each June, athletes come from all over the world to participate in the Cascade Run-Off. More sedentary folks line the streets in lawn chairs and hand out drinks of water to the thirsty runners.

Portland is also the home of the Portland Trailblazers, the 1977 National Basketball Association Champions and a team with a consistent winning tradition. The Portland crowds are renowned for their enthusiastic support of the Blazers, and the coliseum has been sold out for every game for over ten years.

The inspired and the inspirational come together each September for Artquake, a

Saturday Market

Fun for all

(Opposite) *The Herschel Spillman Carousel*

month long exhibit in downtown Portland which showcases hundreds of artists and their varied genres.

The winter months are highlighted by The Parade of Christmas Ships, a breathtaking procession of boats, adorned with shimmering Christmas lights. As they cruise the Willamette and Columbia Rivers, the boats can be viewed from many locations—to the absolute delight of onlookers! Another notable winter exhibit is Peacock Lane, an entire block of homes in Southeast Portland that light up the winter night with their elaborate holiday displays.

On a musical note, April brings with it the Mayor's Ball. Over fifty bands of various types, from rock and roll to jazz to blues, congregate at the Memorial Coliseum to benefit local charities. A single ticket allows the music buff to roam among six separate stages to catch the musical acts of his choice.

Portland has numerous organizations dedicated year-round to celebrating the many faceted dimensions of our culture. A ride on MAX (short for the Metropolitan Area Express) brings you into the downtown core and close to many interesting attractions. The light rail system follows a 15 mile course from Gresham, an eastside suburb, to downtown Portland. Described by Portland Mayor Bud Clark as "a backbone to the whole downtown," MAX is expected to carry 58,000 riders daily by 1995.

Within a few blocks of a MAX station, the Portland Art Museum has an impressive collection of 35 centuries of world art, including Chinese artifacts, Native American art, European impressionism and modern art. Founded in 1892, the museum is one of the oldest on the west coast.

If you are interested in a glimpse into bygone years, a visit to the Oregon Historical Society is in order. This group is devoted to remembering and preserving Oregon's past. The society includes a library, a museum and a revealing photograph collection of nearly two million images which trace Oregon's history! You can spend a rainy afternoon thumbing through time via this extensive photo treasury. Somber faced boys in suspendered shorts, a long ago lumberjack leaning against a slender tree, and a big eyed, bonnet clad baby peeking from her buggy are framed forever within nearly forgotten tintypes. A study of the Oregon Historical Society's photo collection is akin to a trip on a time machine.

The Portland Center for the Performing Arts, completed in 1987, includes a 900 seat theatre with traditional proscenium arch opening, a smaller more casual theatre and the exquisitely restored Arlene Schnitzer Concert Hall. Outside the later, a glittering "PORTLAND" marquee beckons glamorously to passersby. The Center's attractions include ballet, Shakespearean plays, stand-up comedy, opera, rock and jazz concerts; but the performances of the renown Oregon Symphony Orchestra, under the baton of Maestro James DePreist are the deserved favorite of most. At the Performing Arts Center, Portlanders can truly partake of most any form of entertainment ever to grace a stage!

With a rapidly growing reputation as the Northwest hot spot for nightlife, Portland has blues, jazz and rock and roll. Many performers starting in the Rose City have catapulted to stardom.

Portlanders work up quite an appetite with all this fun and excitement, or so it would appear with the number of restaurants in the Rose City. In fact, Portland has more restaurants per capita than any other city in the country! Every type of restaurant imaginable exists in this city.

The historically significant Dan and Louis Oyster Bar is located on a narrow one-way street in the old business section. Although a little off the beaten path it is a tradition for seafood connoiseurs. The Oyster Bar, founded in 1907 by Louis Wachsmuth, is reputed to serve more oysters than any other restaurant on the West Coast. A nautical flavor prevails in the restaurant—designed to resemble the inside of a ship. The knotty pine walls are adorned with Louis' collection of steins, china plates and marine souvenirs, some of which have been displayed—and dusted—for over six decades.

The Old Spaghetti Factory in John's Landing is noted for its economical prices in a grand setting. Overlooking the Willamette River, the gracious restaurant has an imported purple tile roof, ornate antique furniture, plush oriental rugs and sparkling chandeliers. Children gravitate naturally to eat in the retired trolley car which is parked

Sellwood shops

The old and the new

in the middle of the dining area.

Theme restaurants are very popular in Portland, with a wide variety of ambiences from which to choose. You can indulge your appetite in a converted train caboose, or a retired ship floating on the Willamette. You can catch a helicopter to the top of a skyscraper for dinner, or brunch on the working sternwheeler "COLUMBIA GORGE" as it cruises down the river. A wide selection of ethnic, family and elegant restaurants exist to serve the hearty and varied Portland appetite.

If there is one thing that Portlanders enjoy as much as a satisfying meal, it is reading a satisfying book. Perhaps it is the undemanding quality of a rainy Portland day that allows you to feel free to snuggle up on the window seat with a steaming cup of tea, a warm cat curled around your ankles and a nice fat book. It is probably images such as this which contribute to the proliferation of book stores in Portland.

A distinct literary bent exists in Portland, and it is appropriate that one of the largest book stores on the continent is located here. Powell's Book Store, housed in a huge rambling building which spans a whole city block, could supply two books to every resident of the city and still have thousands left over! A special feature of Powell's, the Anne Hughes Coffee Room, focuses on frequent readings by both local and national writers.

It is not surprising that some very fine writers have their roots in Portland. Award-winning children's author Beverly Cleary grew up in Portland and the setting for many of her books is Klickitat Street in northeast Portland. Author Jean Auel lived in Portland while writing her acclaimed *Clan of the Cave Bear.* Walt Morey, author of world famous *Gentle Ben,* resides in the south suburb of Wilsonville. In addition, Portland can claim science fiction author—Ursula K. LeGuin among its famed writers.

Portland, Oregon is a city that reaches for the future as she embraces the past. The burgeoning metropolis has earned a reputation as a recognized force in computer and software technology, and is becoming increasingly important as a national gateway to the Orient. Yet progress has not spoiled this city. She somehow manages to retain the relaxed, small town character that has so endeared her to her residents. Absent is the constant horn honking, impatient shoving in shopping lines and other rude behavior often found in large cities. This city is so charming and comfortable that people are sometimes fooled by the relaxed pace. They don't realize she has come a long way.

Portland, as The Clearing, was like a dozing baby of little consequence. Later, infested with stumps, she was like a gawky, blemished teenager, unsure and mocked by her peers. But she grew from her awkward stage and proved her worth as a mature city. A nationwide study, *Report Card for the 1990's,* confirmed the Rose City's stature. Voted the most underrated city, she garnered top marks for the brightest future and best managed city in the country. From The Clearing, to Stumptown, to the Rose City, Portland has grown into a dynamic reality.

Laurelhurst Park

(Rear Cover) Japanese Gardens in the fall